D1379347

# Lions

by Susan Schafer with Susan M. Meredith

**Marshall Cavendish**
Benchmark
New York

Marshall Cavendish Benchmark
99 White Plains Road
Tarrytown, NY 10591
www.marshallcavendish.us

All websites were available and accurate when this book was sent to press.

Library of Congress Cataloging-in-Publication Data

Schafer, Susan.
   Lions / by Susan Schafer, with Susan Markowitz Meredith.
     p. cm. – (Benchmark rockets. Animals)
   Includes index.
   Summary: "Describes the physical characteristics, habitat, behavior, diet, life cycle, and conservation status of lions"–Provided by publisher.
   ISBN 978-0-7614-4344-5
1.  Lions–Juvenile literature.  I. Meredith, Susan Markowitz. II. Title.

QL737.C23S288 2010
599.757–dc22
2008052104

Publisher: Michelle Bisson
Editorial Development and Book Design: Trillium Publishing, Inc.

Photo research by Trillium Publishing, Inc.

Cover photo: Shutterstock.com/Keith Levit

The photographs and illustrations in this book are used by permission and through the courtesy of: *iStockphoto.com*: Marek Dziok, 1; Kristian Sekulic, 4–5; aldra, 6; Brian Raisbeck, 8–9; zmajdoo, 12 (top); Henri Faure, 14–15; Peter Malsbury, 17. *Marshall Cavendish Benchmark*: 7. *Shutterstock.com*: Johan Swanepoel, 10; David Peta, 11; Steffen Foerster Photography, 12 (bottom); Sandro V. Maduell, 13; Helicestudio, 16. *AP Photo*: Karel Prinsloo, 18–19; Sayyid Azim, 21. *Sunny Gagliano*: 20.

Printed in Malaysia
1 3 5 6 4 2

# Contents

This male African lion watches over the other lions.

## Chapter 1

# The King of Beasts

There are two kinds of lions—the African lion and the Asian lion. Lions belong to the animal group called "big cats." Tigers, leopards, and cheetahs are in this group, too. Big cats live in many places. Some live in rain forests. Others live on the plains. Still other big cats make their home in the mountains.

Lions are different from other big cats. Their fur is a smooth, dark yellow. Most other big cats have spots or stripes. The lion's tail is different, too. There is black fur on the tip. Even the male lion's neck is different. It has long fur around it called a mane.

Lions live in groups called prides.

Lions live in a family called a **pride**. The lions in a pride work together to hunt for food and protect each other. No other big cat lives this way.

A pride of lions may have up to 20 adult lions. Most of the adults are female. They are called lionesses. Many **cubs** live in the pride, too. The place where each pride lives is its **territory**. The territory may be small if it has plenty of food for the pride. If there is not a lot of food, the pride must travel far to find some. Then the territory is large.

The strongest male lion is always the king of the pride. The other males help him protect the group. Males are made for fighting. A male lion can weigh 400 to 500 pounds (180–225 kilograms). He may be over 9 feet (2.8 meters) long, too. He may be 3.5 feet (1 m) high at the shoulder.

Female lions are smaller than males. A lioness may weigh 275 to 300 pounds (125–135 kg). Lionesses are good hunters. They catch food for the whole pride.

Male lions are larger than females. They have long fur around the neck.

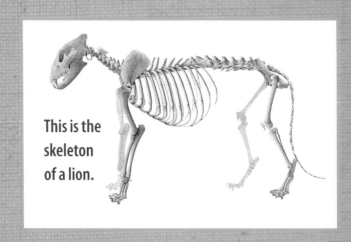
This is the skeleton of a lion.

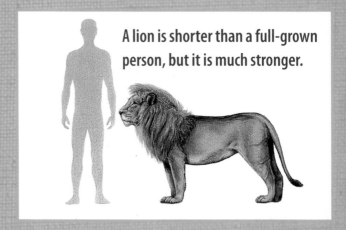
A lion is shorter than a full-grown person, but it is much stronger.

Animals like these wildebeest feed on the savannah all day long. They are prey for lions.

## Chapter 2
# A Hunting Life

Most of the world's lions live on the African **savannah**. The savannah is a grassland that goes on for miles and miles. There are only a few trees here and there. The savannah is dry most of the time, but it has a short rainy season. Then for several weeks, the grass gets very green.

African lions live on the savannah all year long. Sometimes a pride finds water on the savannah's edges where bushes and trees grow. The lions can keep cool in the shade.

The pride does its hunting on the grassland. The land is flat, so the lions can watch groups of animals like zebras

**A lioness stalks her prey.**

and buffalo eating grass. These grass-eaters are the lions' **prey**. They provide food for the pride. The African savannah has the most grass-eaters in the world.

Lions work together to hunt for prey. One lioness hides in some tall brown grass on one side of a herd of zebras. Her fur blends right in with the grass so the herd doesn't see her. The wind blows her smell away so they don't smell her, either. The lioness is still and quiet. She waits. Her eyes never leave the zebras.

Five other lionesses go to the other side of the zebras. They also wait in the tall grass. Then they step into view, walking side by side.

A zebra sees the lionesses and makes a noise a bit like the bark of a dog to warn the other zebras. The zebras are afraid and start to move away.

The zebras don't know what is in front of them. They are walking straight toward the hiding lioness!

All of a sudden, the five lionesses rush at the zebras. The zebras leap forward. They think all the hunters are behind them.

One zebra is slower than the rest. It runs toward the lioness hiding in the grass. Now the lioness leaps from the grass. She grabs for the

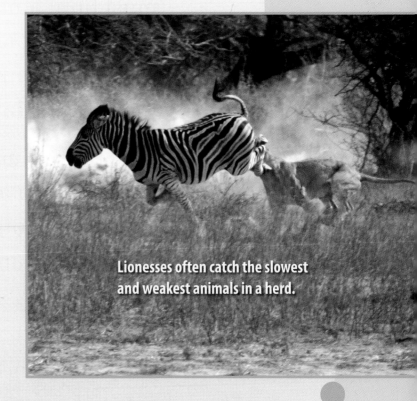

Lionesses often catch the slowest and weakest animals in a herd.

zebra's neck, but she misses. Then she catches its leg. But the zebra kicks hard. It breaks free and runs away.

The lioness does not follow. Lions catch their prey by **ambush**, not running. The team of lionesses will move to a new place. Maybe there they will find their next meal.

11

Female lions miss more animals than they catch. This means that they must hunt almost every day or night. Sometimes it takes two to three days to find food. Sometimes they steal food from another **predator**.

The pride is always hungry and ready to eat. They rush for the food. They hiss and fight with each other as each one tries to eat as much as it can. Male lions take the most. A big male might eat 90 pounds (40 kg) of food at one time.

The hungry cubs want food, too. But they wait until the adults are done. Cubs can get hurt if they do not wait their turn.

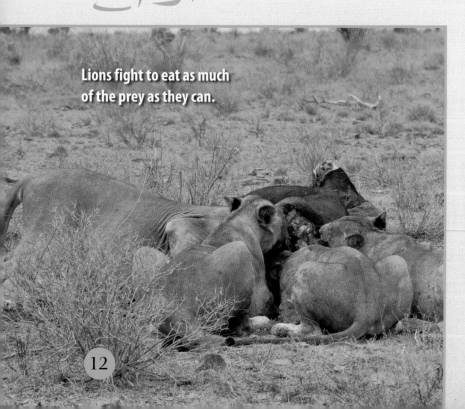

Lions fight to eat as much of the prey as they can.

After eating, the pride sits down. Each lion licks its face and paws. The lions clean each other, too. Their tongues work like brushes.

Soon the lions feel sleepy. They stretch out and yawn. These hunters are ready for a nap. They like to cuddle, so they rest with their heads on each other.

Lions sleep up to 22 hours a day. They save their energy for hunting.

A lioness and her cubs blend in with the yellow grass.

## Chapter 3

# Growing Up Lion

A lioness knows when it is time to **mate**. She walks up to the king of the pride. He will be the father. Three months later the lioness is ready to give birth.

The lioness leaves the pride to find a hiding place near large rocks or bushes. There, she gives birth to two or three cubs. A cub weighs about 3 pounds (1.5 kg). Each cub has spots on its fur. The spots help the cubs blend in with the land. Predators often walk right by the cubs without seeing them.

The lioness feeds and cleans her babies. She leaves them only when she needs to drink and hunt for food.

15

After about two weeks, the cubs open their eyes. Soon they begin walking and playing together. They don't go far from home. Their mother is not always there to protect them. They may need to get back to their hiding place fast.

After two months, the cubs have strong legs. They follow their mother back to the pride. Many other cubs are there, too. Their mothers gave birth around the same time so that all the mothers can help each other care for the young.

Two cubs wait for their mother to return from the hunt.

At six months, the cubs are one-fourth the size of an adult lion. They are too small to join a hunt, but they play hunting games every day. They chase the tails of adults. They jump on each other. They wrestle and bite and grab leaves in the air. The adult males watch over the cubs.

Sometimes the males roar loudly so other predators know to stay away.

The growing cubs watch the lionesses hunt. They are ready to join the hunt when they are about a year old. They are ready to live on their own at two to three years.

The female lions stay with the pride, but the young males do not. They join other young males and **roam** the plains. When a male lion is strong enough, he will fight for a pride of his own. If he wins, he will be the new king.

The winner of this fight will become king of the pride.

When a young male wins a pride, the old king must leave. He goes back to the plains to roam once more. He will never go back to his pride.

17

People and cattle are moving into places where African lions live.

## Chapter 4
# Losing Ground

Lions once roamed in many parts of the world before people began killing them. In 1913, there were only 20 Asian lions left. Now they are protected and only live in one part of India. Little by little, more Asian lion cubs are being born. Still, these lions are **endangered** and may not **survive**.

African lions are a little better off. Today, some of the savannah is protected. Many African lions now live in national parks and **game reserves**.

But people are still a problem for African lions. People build houses and farms where lions live. They let their cattle graze on the savannah.

Wild animals like zebras and buffalo leave because they have no food to eat. Without the wild herds of grass-eaters, lions have no food, either. Sometimes the hungry lions kill cattle. Then people often get angry and kill the lions.

## Where Lions Live

Lions used to roam in large areas. But today they have less room to live. The African lion's habitat is much smaller now. The Asian lion lives only in a tiny area in India.

EUROPE

ASIA

AFRICA

Past Habitat

Present Habitat

People harm African lions in other ways. Some hunters kill lions for fun. They want to bring home a lion's skin or head. Some people even kill lions that are protected. This is called **poaching**. It's against the law.

Still, many people want to save the lions. Some people try to stop the **poachers**. Some work to stop the spread of sickness among lions. And some teach children and adults to help wild animals such as lions.

People are working together to save the prides of Africa. They can save the savannah, too. Only then will the lion live on as king of the animals.

The mother of these lion cubs died. Now people at the Nairobi Animal Orphanage in Kenya take care of them.

# Glossary

**ambush:** A surprise attack.

**cubs:** The young of certain animals, such as lions.

**endangered:** At risk of becoming extinct, or dying off forever.

**game reserves:** Places set aside just for wild animals to live.

**mate:** When a male and female join as a pair in order to produce young.

**poaching:** Killing animals that are protected. **Poachers** are people who go against the law by hunting or fishing in a place where animals are protected.

**predator:** An animal that lives by killing and eating other animals.

**prey:** Animals hunted for food by other animals. Zebras are lions' prey.

**pride:** A group of lions that lives together.

**roam:** To move around from place to place.

**savannah:** An open grassland with trees or shrubs here and there.

**survive:** To stay alive.

**territory:** The area chosen by an animal or group of animals as its own.

# Find Out More

## Books

Anderson, Jill. *Lions*. New York: Northword Books for Young Readers, 2006.

Joubert, Dereck. *Face to Face with Lions*. Washington, D.C.: National Geographic Children's Books, 2008.

Schafer, Susan. *Lions* (Animals Animals). New York: Marshall Cavendish, 2001.

Squire, Ann O. *Lions*. New York: Scholastic Children's Press, 2008.

Stefoff, Rebecca. *Lions* (AnimalWays). New York: Marshall Cavendish, 2006.

## Websites

African Wildlife Foundation
http://www.awf.org/content/wildlife/detail/lion

Asiatic Lion Information Centre
http://www.asiatic-lion.org

The Kingdom of Lions
http://home.worldonline.nl/~rlion/lkindex.htm

National Geographic Kids
http://kids.nationalgeographic.com/Animals/CreatureFeature/Lion

# Index

Page numbers for photographs and illustrations are in **boldface**.